W9-ACK-285

MAY 0 3 2010

Vietnam War
MEMORIAL

J.S. Burrows

ROURKE PUBLISHING

Vero Beach, Florida 32964

www.rourkepublishing.com

Photo credits: © U.S. Department of Defense: Title Page, 11, 13, 17, 19, 20, 21, 23, 26, 27; © Nick Edens: 5; © U.S. Air Force: 6; © Associated Press: 7, 8, 15, 28; © dejan suc: 9; © Wikipedia: 12; © Rob Meeske: 14; © Jim Cassatt: 16; © Michelle Malven: 25

Editor: Kelli Hicks

Cover and Interior design by Tara Raymo

Library of Congress Cataloging-in-Publication Data

Burrows, Jennifer.
  Vietnam War Memorial / Jennifer Burrows.
    p. cm. -- (War memorials)
  Includes index.
  ISBN 978-1-60694-424-0
  1. Vietnam Veterans Memorial (Washington, D.C.)--Juvenile literature. 2.
Vietnam War, 1961-1975--United States--Juvenile literature. 3. Washington
(D.C.)--Buildings, structures, etc.--Juvenile literature. I. Title.
  DS559.83.W18B87 2010
  959.704'36--dc22
                                    2009006012

Printed in the USA

CG/CG

ROURKE PUBLISHING

www.rourkepublishing.com - rourke@rourkepublishing.com
Post Office Box 643328 Vero Beach, Florida 32964

Table of Contents

The Vietnam Veterans Memorial

After many American wars, our soldiers returned home as heroes. When the soldiers came home from the Vietnam War, they did not feel like heroes. Many Americans treated them poorly and unfairly.

About ten years after the war, a small group of people wanted to honor the Vietnam **veterans** with a memorial. They created the Vietnam Veterans **Memorial** as a **tribute** to the American men and women who served in the Vietnam War.

The memorial is located on the National Mall. The National Mall is two miles of land between the Lincoln Memorial and the Capitol in Washington, D.C.

The Vietnam Veteran's Memorial recently received an award for being the most-visited monument in Washington, D.C.

The Vietnam War

In 1957, North Vietnam attacked South Vietnam. The United States tried to help South Vietnam because the U.S. wanted to stop the spread of **Communism.** North Vietnam was a **Communist** country and South Vietnam was not.

By the 1960s, many American troops were in Vietnam. Some Americans supported the war, but many did not. The United States became badly divided over the war.

Although many people throughout the nation held strong views opposing the war, families were overjoyed when their loved ones returned home.

Mongolia

China

Nepal

Bhutan

ndia

Pakistan

Burma

Bay
of Bengal

Laos

North
Vietnam

South
Vietnam

Thailand

Cambodia

Gulf of
Thailand

Andaman
Sea

South China
Sea

Philippi

Halong Bay,
Vietnam

ppine
Sea

Palau

i Lanka

a n

Malaysia

Singapore

Brunei

Malaysia

Indonesia

New Gui

Java Sea

East Timor

Sea of

Pacific O

North and South Vietnam are in Southeast Asia. Together, they are
about the same size as New Mexico. Both countries have many
mountains and forests.

Creating the Vietnam Veterans Memorial

Jan Scruggs fought in the Vietnam War for over a year. He wanted the names of the Americans who died or didn't return from battle to be written on a memorial. Mr. Scruggs also wanted to help the United States heal from the division over the war.

Fellow veterans, Bob Doubek and John Wheeler, joined Mr. Scruggs and they started the Vietnam Veterans Memorial Fund. They got support from people who were both for and against the Vietnam War. Everyone put aside their different opinions and worked together to honor the American men and women who served.

While serving as the founder and president of the Vietnam Veterans Memorial Fund, Mr. Jan Scruggs, pictured above, often spoke to groups to gain support and funding to build the memorial.

Design submitted by Maya Lin

The Vietnam Veterans Memorial Fund held a contest to design the memorial. A graduate student named Maya Lin won. She designed a memorial to look like the ground had been cut open and then healed over, like a scar in the earth.

Some people didn't like Miss Lin's design. As a **compromise**, a statue and an American flag became part of the design.

The Parts of the Memorial

A shiny, black **granite** wall **gradually** rises and falls back into the earth at the Vietnam Veterans Memorial. The Wall is shaped like a wide V. It is shorter at the ends and taller in the middle. The Wall is about 500 feet (152 meters) long.

More than 58,000 names are carved into the **glossy** surface of the Wall. The names are in the order that they died or didn't return from battle during the Vietnam War.

Since 1983, an American flag and flagpole are also a part of the memorial. The flag flies 24 hours a day, seven days a week.

Two small models of the Wall travel around the United States.

A bronze statue of three American soldiers became part of the memorial on Veteran's Day, 1984. It is called The Three Servicemen Statue. An artist named Frederick Hart designed and **sculpted** the statue.

The statue shows the closeness and trust of the soldiers who fought in the Vietnam War.

The statues look in the direction of the Wall as if they are searching for the name of a friend.

Another bronze statue of three nurses helping a wounded soldier became a part of the memorial in 1993. It is called the Vietnam Women's Memorial. An artist named Glenna Goodacre designed and sculpted the statue.

The statue shows the commitment and kindness of the women who served in the Vietnam War.

A website called The Virtual Wall started in 1998. The website has information about the memorial and more. Many veterans and their loved ones keep in touch through the website.

A National Salute to Vietnam Veterans

On November 10, 1982, there was a candlelight service at the National Cathedral in Washington, D.C. The original 57,939 names engraved on the Wall were read.

On November 11 and 12 of that same year, there were workshops, ceremonies, receptions, reunions, and entertainment for the Vietnam veterans.

More than three million Americans served in the Vietnam War.

On November 13, there was a Vietnam Victory Parade. Over 15,000 Vietnam veterans marched down Constitution Avenue in Washington, D.C.

Following the parade was the dedication of the memorial. About 150,000 people gathered on the National Mall that day.

The National **Salute** ended on November 14 with religious services all over the country remembering Vietnam veterans.

Visiting the Wall is a moving experience for people of all ages. For many it provides an opportunity to connect with family members they never knew.

So Many Visitors

Four million people visit the Vietnam Veterans Memorial each year. Both young and old come at all times of the day, in any weather, and in all four seasons of the year.

Some visitors salute, some stare, some take pictures, and many cry. Most touch the Wall as they read the names written on their own reflections.

The ground around the Wall is usually scattered with notes, flowers, and special objects. Each day the items left to commemorate the veterans are gathered and put in the Vietnam Veterans Memorial Collection. The collection has over 100,000 items in it. Many of these items will eventually be permanently displayed in the underground education center planned for the memorial.

The Vietnam Veterans Memorial helped to heal a nation. It thanked the veterans of the Vietnam War and finally honored them as heroes. Mr. Scruggs said, "America's Vietnam veterans were finally welcomed home."

Timeline

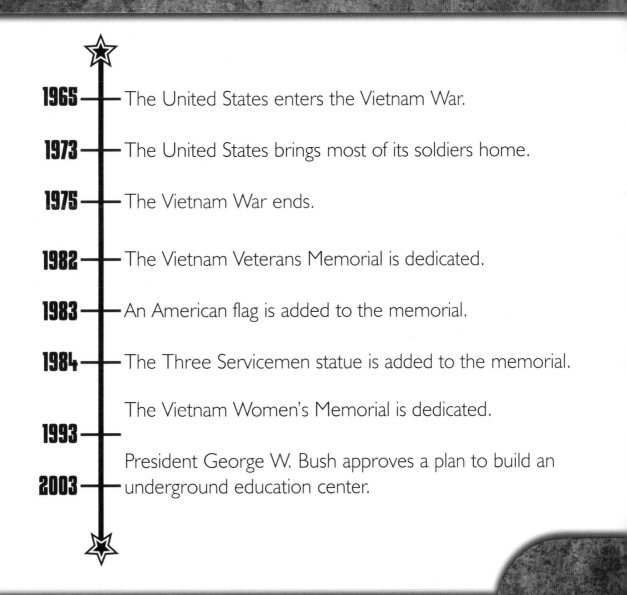

1965 — The United States enters the Vietnam War.

1973 — The United States brings most of its soldiers home.

1975 — The Vietnam War ends.

1982 — The Vietnam Veterans Memorial is dedicated.

1983 — An American flag is added to the memorial.

1984 — The Three Servicemen statue is added to the memorial.

1993 — The Vietnam Women's Memorial is dedicated.

2003 — President George W. Bush approves a plan to build an underground education center.

Interesting Facts

Maya Lin was a student at Yale University when she entered the design contest. Her design started as homework. She got a B on the assignment.

Many states have memorials dedicated to local Vietnam veterans.

★ One in Tallahassee, Florida, consists of two granite columns with an American flag hanging between them.

★ In Troy, New York, there is a ten foot (three meter) bronze statue of three soldiers.

★ San Antonio, Texas, has a ten foot (three meter) bronze sculpture of a radio operator comforting an injured friend.

★ In Springfield, Illinois, there is an eternal flame held up by five gray granite walls.

★ In Sacramento, California, there are five bronze sculptures showing life during the Vietnam War.

Glossary

compromise (KOM-pruh-mize): to agree to something that is not exactly what you want

Communism (KOM-yuh-niz-uhm): a system of organizing a country so that the people share all of their resources under the government's control

Communist (KOM-yuh-nist): a person or group of people who follow Communism

glossy (GLAWSS-ee): shiny surface

gradually (GRAJ-yoo-uhl-ee): slowly, but steadily

granite (GRAN-it): a type of rock

memorial (muh-MOR-ee-uhl): something built to help people remember a person or an event

salute (suh-LOOT): to praise or honor someone or to raise your right hand to your forehead as a sign of respect

sculpted (SKUHLP-ted): carved

tribute (TRIB-yoot): a show of thanks or respect

veterans (VET-ur-uhn): people who have served in the armed forces, especially during a war

Index

Websites

www.thevirtualwall.org
www.thewall-usa.com
www.nps.gov/vive
www.tourofdc.org/monuments/VVM
go.footnote.com/thewall
www.vietvet.org/thewall.htm

About the Author

J. S. Burrows is a former teacher who
loves writing stories for children. She is
deeply patriotic and thinks the men and
women who serve in the military are
heroes. When she's not writing, she
enjoys cooking and playing Dance
        Dance Revolution with her
            three kids.